BOO

Written
Translated

The Maids

BY JEAN GENET

BrightSummaries.com

JEAN GENET

WRITER, POET, AND PLAYWRIGHT

- **Born in Paris in 1910**
- **Died there in 1986**
- **Notable works:**
  - *Our Lady of the Flowers* (1944), novel
  - *The Maids* (1947) play
  - *Querelle of Brest* (1947) novel

Jean Genet was born in Paris on 19th December 1910. Abandoned by his mother, he began committing theft when he was a teenager, a time during which he also discovered his homosexuality. He was sent to the penal colony of Mettray, before enrolling in the Foreign Legion, which he deserted to lead the life of a thief, a beggar and a prostitute. He started writing in prison and, in 1942, while he was imprisoned at Fresnes, he published his first poem, *The Man Sentenced to Death*. He then produced autobiographical novels, such as *The Miracle of the Rose*. In the 1960s, he became well-known for his theatrical works: his plays *The Maids* and *The Screens* were hugely successful. He was encouraged by Jean Cocteau and Jean-Paul Sartre. In 1983, he was awarded the Grand Prix national des Lettres. He died on 15th April 1986 from a fatal fall down the stairs.

THE MAIDS

A PLAY INSPIRED BY A NEWS ITEM

- **Genre:** play
- **Reference edition:** Genet, J. (2012) *Les Bonnes*. Paris: Gallimard.[1]
- **First edition:** 1947
- **Themes:** murder, identity, game, submission, jealousy, fratricide

The play *The Maids* was inspired by a sordid news item: the murder of their employer by the Papin sisters in 1933. Jean Genet took inspiration from this wild crime, perpetrated without any apparent motive, to invent the story of two maids, Claire and Solange, sisters who repeat the same ritual each night: they pretend to strangle their employer. But one day, the comedy turns into a tragedy and the two young women find themselves the prisoners of their own game. This tragic work can be seen as a practical application of the Theatre of Cruelty, a theatrical theory developed by Antonin Artaud. Jean Genet constantly rewrote his play between July 1946, when he met stage director Louis Jouvet, and April 1947, when the work was first performed at the Théâtre de l'Athénée.

1. Quotes taken from the reference edition have been translated by BrightSummaries.com.

SUMMARY

The entire play takes place in Madame's bedchamber, a baroque room filled with flowers and furnished in a Louis XV style.

MURDER GAME

In their mistress' absence, two sisters, who are working as maids, take part each evening in a role play, which has become a real ritual for them. Claire, the youngest and frailest of the two sisters, becomes Madame, while Solange, the oldest and most violent, becomes Claire. This trivial and scathing comedy shows the ambiguous relationships of the two women with their employer. The false Madame despises her maid. She constantly talks down to her ("I will be beautiful. More than you will ever be. Because it is not with that body and that face that you will seduce Mario" p.18), she calls her "a fool" (p.18). Though the maid shows respect and obedience at first, declaring "I love you" (p.22), she is quickly overcome by feelings of hatred, and ends up insulting and threatening her employer: "I hate you! I despise you. You no longer frighten me." (p. 28). It is a complex relationship made of love and hatred, admiration and jealousy, dependence and disdain.

This role play is terribly ambiguous, because it is unclear whether it is Madame picking on her maids, whether it is the maid who is rebelling, or whether the two sisters are manifesting their own differences. Moreover, Solange plays the role of herself as well as that of her younger sister. As for Claire, when she confesses to having reported Monsieur, Madame's lover, to the police for theft, the two opposite viewpoints of the mistress and the maid mingle and intermingle in total confusion, making the actress' speech seem perfectly incoherent. However, behind this game of make-believe, the real feelings of the two sisters are shown. Behind their apparent complicity hides a fratricidal struggle.

Indeed, through the letter of denunciation that she writes, probably out of jealousy, Claire is trying to have Monsieur imprisoned, which would cause not only Madame's unhappiness, but also that of Solange, as she is love with him. Several times, Mario the milkman is also mentioned, whose nocturnal visits trigger the erotic fantasies of the two sisters, as well as scenes of jealousy between them. Claire, playing Madame, pretending to be the suffering lover, wants to put on Madame's white gown, because of the color worn by queens in mourning, but Solange refuses and becomes completely hysterical. The reader can see a real settling of accounts in the family. Moreover, Solange admits failing in her attempts to kill Madame, which her younger sister berates her for. While she is on the verge of strangling her false employer - her own sister - an alarm clock sounds, signaling that it is time for them to tidy everything up before Madame's return. This murder game is actually a prefiguration of what is about to happen.

Suddenly, the telephone rings: it is Monsieur, who has just been granted interim release and meets Madame at the Bilboquet. This unexpected development disrupts everything, because in a few hours, Madame and Monsieur will discover that it was Claire who wrote the denunciation letter. The two sisters thus find themselves at a dead end: they can no longer turn back.

PREPARING FOR MURDER

Monsieur's release precipitates everything. The two maids understand that they will soon be confronted and that it is therefore necessary to kill Madame: Solange and Claire chose to poison her by putting gardenal (a barbiturate) in her linden-tee. Claire prepares the brew.

At that moment, Madame comes in, dressed in fur. With a nervous laugh, she first laments her fate and declares herself ready to follow Monsieur to prison, like a romantic heroine. She then calms down and considers a retirement in the countryside, with her maids, not talking about Monsieur anymore. In an outburst of tenderness and generosity, she then gifts her own dresses to her two maids, who initially refuse, before accepting them, fascinated by these precious gifts. Madame refuses the herbal tea offered to her with insistence and finally discovers that the phone has been taken off the hook: the maids are forced to confess that Monsieur has called. After this revelation, Madame's bourgeois side resurfaces, and she gives orders to her maids so that she can be reunited with her lover more quickly. While Solange goes to fetch a cab, Madame notices that the alarm clock is in the room and that Claire is wearing makeup. Impatient, she finally flees without drinking her herbal tea and without being alarmed by the details she notices.

Alone again, the maids find themselves in a difficult situation. Solange reproaches her sister for not having forced Madame to drink the poison. Trapped by her sister's recriminations, Claire becomes Madame again. Solange then becomes violently mad and launches into a long monologue. She leaps on Claire to strangle her. Believing that she has killed Madame, the eldest of the two maids continues her monologue in a hallucination of triumph, imagining herself to be Madame mourning her maid. But Claire comes back to life, like the living-dead, to put an end to her sister's black mass. Once her elation is suppressed, Claire takes control of the game and pushes Solange towards murder. Solange finally obeys and poisons her own sister. The game has ended with their downfall: Madame is alive, Monsieur is free, Claire has been poisoned by her own sister and Solange will be sent to the gallows.

CHARACTER STUDY

THE MAIDS

The main characters are characterized by their role, their function: Solange and Claire are servants. As highlighted by the title, the two maids are one entity, they are inseparable and intrinsically linked. Claire represents the light and clear-sightedness, and the same goes for Solange, whose name also has a celestial and solar connotation. However, the choice of these names actually seems ironic, as both sisters are fatal characters and bearers of death.

Nonetheless, this couple is imbalanced, as far as their personalities are concerned: Claire, the youngest, is afraid of her older sister, Solange, who is more violent and more exalted. However, during their game, Claire, embodying Madame, becomes demanding, far from her usually shy and gentle nature. The almost incestuous relation of the two women is perturbed by erotic evocations of Monsieur and Mario the milkman, which triggers a settling of accounts between Solange and Claire. Their feelings towards each other are defined by their dependency, or even their alienation: one cannot exist without the other. Moreover, the two sisters reflect each other as in a game of mirrors. They are therefore interchangeable, to the point where Madame herself mixes them up and where, during their little play, Solange plays both her own role and that of her sister.

MADAME

This character is the embodiment of the bourgeoisie. Moreover, Genet did not even give her a proper name, as if he was trying to confine her to that category. From her clothes, her expressions and her behavior, this woman seems vain and superficial. However, even though she overstates her despair and sufferings, she remains a strict employer who observes her employees' behavior and the position of objects with precision. She is therefore on the verge of discovering her maids' game, but her excitement at the idea of seeing Monsieur again takes over her mind, and she accepts Claire's rather unconvincing explanations without further questioning.

ANALYSIS

THE DOUBLE

The theme of the double structures the whole play. Indeed, as mentioned above, the two maids are almost interchangeable, so much so that Madame mixes them up. Moreover, there is confusion as to their identities, from the beginning of the text onwards. It is hard to determine who plays whom, like Claire who, playing Madame, hesitates between two names, not knowing which role Solange is playing anymore; "CLAIRE, *murmuring*.- Claire, Solange, Claire." (p. 29). This theatrical game in the play involves an unavoidable discrepancy between the reader and the spectator. The first, warned by the stage directions and presentation of the dialogues, understands more quickly that it is a comedy, while the spectator, without any tangible benchmarks, doubts and mixes the two young women up.

During this acting game, Solange gives Claire a mirror so that she can watch herself playing Madame. Claire then admires herself in a narcissistic fashion, finding herself beautiful, and even denying her own identity: "CLAIRE, *looking at herself with approval*. I am more beautiful in there! Danger surrounds me like a halo, Claire, whereas you are only darkness..." (p.30). This accessory, which is highly symbolic, therefore suggests the psychic duality of the character and, at the same time, poses the problem of alterity, clearly referring us back to recognition theory, illustrated by the famous dialectic of the master and the slave of the German philosopher Georg Wilhelm Friedrich Hegel (1770-1831).

Genet's maids have a conflictual relationship, because they cannot be independent and autonomous. They have only reached the first stage of Hegel's recognition, which is the stage of alienation: they depend on each other. This stage corresponds to narcissistic love, which consists of the negation of the other who is then used simply as a mirror. Claire both hates and loves the image of herself that Solange offers, and vice-versa. But the two women are also dependent on their mistress, and this is what is implicitly acted out in this initial role play. They only exist as maids and as sisters through the eyes of Madame, and conversely, Madame only exists as a mistress because of the maids. Each is the mirror of the others. This is coherent with Hegelian philosophy, except that in Genet's work, the maids never reach the stage of self-awareness. They remain at the stage of the struggle for recognition, each of them wishing to be consciously perceived as independent and unique. The entire play showcases the incapacity of these two women to become independent from each other and to exist outside of a dependent relationship – dependent between sisters, but also between master and servant. The mirror object thus suggests a philosophical and psychoanalytical reading of the play – Hegelian philosophy is echoed in psychoanalysis through the concept of the mirror stage, developed by Lacan (French psychiatrist and psychoanalyst, 1901-1981) among others.

GOOD TO KNOW: THE HEGELIAN DIALECTIC OF MASTER AND SLAVE

It is in the *Phenomenology of Spirit* that Hegel discusses

his theory of recognition, illustrated by the dialectic of the master and the slave.

According to Hegel, for the subject to become aware of himself, he must first distinguish his 'Me' from that of others, which means that self-recognition does imply reciprocity. To illustrate this theory, Hegel chose to study the relationship of domination between master and slave.

The recognition of these two beings is at first unilateral, because the master recognizes himself through the orders he gives and can therefore see himself act through his slave as though through a mirror. But the master also depends on the slave, because he needs the latter to feel himself exist. In a way, the slave thus becomes his master's master, his own conscience. He also manages to become aware of himself through his work, as he transforms matter and recognizes his own works. As the process of recognition happens, the master therefore becomes dependent while the slave acquires a certain form of autonomy - which should not be mistaken for the idea of freedom.

These ambivalent feelings which tie the three women together are translated in the scenography through the choice of costumes. The dresses clearly mark the social distinction between the mistress of the house and her employees. But, as soon as the maids put on these same dresses, their identities are blurred.

This confusion can also be found in the symbolism of colors, as each dress color has its own connotations. For example, white refers to the Assumption, the immaculate innocence and death, as it is the color of royal mourning, suggesting the idea of rebirth. Red, on the other hand, denotes both desire and blood - Solange puts on the red dress of the strangler during her monologue.

A COMPLEX STRUCTURE

At first glance, The Maids appears as a classical play, considering that the rule of three unities is followed. There is indeed a unity of action - killing Madame -, a unity of time – the play takes place over one evening - and a unity of place, as it all happens in Madame's bedchamber. This room is actually a perfect place for closed proceedings: from the décor alone, an atmosphere of stuffiness permeates everything, exacerbating passion. Moreover, although the play is not divided into acts or scenes, some have seen in Genet's text a five-act structure worthy of a classical tragedy.

However, all comparison with the classical canon ends there, as Genet plays out theatrical conventions. The first part of the play corresponds to a sort of anti-exposition, with the role play of the two maids. Although the reader has the benefit of more information than the spectator, several clues, interspersed here and there, aim to make the audience aware of the artificiality of what happens on stage: confusion with the names, reversals of the power relationship and the behaviors, sentences with double meanings, etc.

The exposure, in the real sense, only happens after the alarm goes off, once the audience understands who the young women on stage really are. With this theatrical play within a play, Genet blurs the borders between reality and illusion. He indirectly denounces the game of make-believe which constitutes any theatrical representation. In addition, he insists on the cyclical nature of theatre, an art that is repeated every night, as the maids play the same game every day. This repetitive temporality implies an idea of fatality. The whole play thus functions as an inevitable march towards death.

THEATRE OF CRUELTY

Each night, the maids re-enact Madame's murder in a neurotic ritual. The room, full of flowers, resembles a tomb and is bathed in a morbid atmosphere, so that the tragedy borders on a surreal and fantastic world. The spectator attends a ceremony, a black mass, which culminates in Solange's monologue with Madame who appears as a living-dead.

The maids should certainly not be read as a realistic play, nor as a social criticism of the servants' submission to their master. Rather, Genet is trying to denounce the scene as being a place of illusion. Through this theatrical play within a play, he pushes the spectator to look beyond appearances and pretenses. The décor of the room tips us over to the side of dreams and human sub-consciousness. The aim is to discover the true nature of the maids and to bring their masochistic and deadly drives to light. In this enclosed space, violence is both physical - attempts at strangling - and moral - wish for death, neurotic jealousy, hallucinations, incest.

The Maids can ultimately be said to be an illustration of the Theatre of Cruelty. Genet rejects the notion that theatre can imitate life and reality. Like Antonin Artaud (French writer, 1896-1948), he tries to project our psyche on stage, in order to unveil the true nature of man, which is violent, neurotic, and cruel. The representation is thought of as a ceremony, a liturgical act in which the spectator communes with his alterity, his other, his double, embodied by the actor on stage.

Good to know: Antonin Artaud's Theater of Cruelty

Antonin Artaud presents a theory which he calls the "Theater of Cruelty" in an essay titled *The Theater and its Double*, published in 1935. Influenced by surrealism and the oriental dramaturgies, he questions the text and the traditional play of the actors, in search of a new theatrical language. In his opinion, the stage is not the place where a representation happens, but should be the place where life is caught in its less representable form. Theater should show the moments of extreme tension, which man always tries to suppress. It is in this sense that Antonin Artaud speaks of "cruelty". We should go back to the etymological meaning of the word, from the Latin *cruor* meaning blood, tortured bodies. Cruelty runs through our blood, meaning both our carnal and latent drives as well as a deep wound to the soul. Artaud's theory is therefore mainly metaphysical, the aim being to project the human subconscious on stage in order to better understand it.

FURTHER REFLECTION

SOME QUESTIONS TO THINK ABOUT...

- Describe the complex relationship between the two maids.
- Why are the characters mainly identified by common names, as reminders of their functions and social status?
- What is the importance of the mirror motif in the work's economy?
- What does the décor symbolize? In your opinion, why did Genet choose only one setting?
- The maids call their role play a 'ceremony'. Explain all the meanings of this word.
- How does Genet seek to provoke unease in the spectator?
- Demonstrate how the play has a cyclical structure. In what way does the ending close the initial ceremony? How is it interesting to open and close the play on a theatrical game within the theatre?
- How does the theatrical game within the theatre allow for a reversal of roles?
- Discuss the evolution of the master/valet couple in theatre, from the Middle-Ages to the 20th century. Are Genet's characters involved in this evolution?
- Explain why this play is a march towards death.
- Is *The Maids* a classical play?
- How does Genet's play illustrate Antonin Artaud's theory of the Theater of Cruelty?
- Compare this work with other plays by Genet (*The Screens*, *The Blacks*, etc.): what are the similarities between these works?

We want to hear from you!
Leave a comment on your online library
and share your favourite books on social media!

FURTHER READING

REFERENCE EDITION

- Genet, J. (2012) *Les Bonnes*. Paris: Gallimard.

www.brightsummaries.com

Ebook EAN: 9782806270382

Paperback EAN: 9782806272133

Legal Deposit: D/2015/12603/540

Digital conception by Primento, the digital partner of publishers.

19577731R00016

Printed in Poland
by Amazon Fulfillment
Poland Sp. z o.o., Wrocław